Contents an

This book will introduce the following:

4-5   **verbs** .... name an action and can also be called 'doing' words

6-7   **auxiliary verbs** ..... like 'be' and 'have', show different forms of the same verb

8-9   **subject** .... tells you who, or what, is doing the action

8-9   **object** .... comes after the verb and tells us who or what is receiving the action of the verb

10-11   **first person** .... means 'I' or 'we' – eg. I am writing in my book

10-11   **second person** ..... means 'you' – eg. You are writing in your book

10-11   **third person** .... means 'he', 'she' or 'they' – eg. He is writing in his book

12-13   **commas** .... separate things in a list and show a pause in a sentence

12-13   **speech marks** ...... show when a person is speaking and can also be called inverted commas

14-15   **adverbs** .... give more information about the verb, telling you when, where or how something is done

Verbs

A **verb** names an **action**.
It can be called a
'doing word'.

Tick all the **verbs** below as you spot them happening in the picture.

run	☐	hop	☐	clap	☐
jump	☐	wave	☐	skip	☐
sit	☐	walk	☐	stand	☐

Write down some **actions** you do every day. These are all **verbs.**

_____

_____

_____

Verbs can also describe how a person or thing is **feeling**.

Use the **verbs** 'want' and 'like' to finish these sentences. Say the sentences out loud to help you.

I _____ a dog.

I _____ dogs.

Can you find these **verbs** in this word search?

paint   sing
know   sleep
eat   play
dig   fly
think

a	t	s	l	e	e	p
t	l	f	s	g	a	l
h	p	a	i	n	t	a
i	y	e	n	f	l	y
n	d	i	g	e	a	f
k	n	o	w	f	e	y

Well done!

Auxiliary verbs

The **verb** 'be' can act as an **auxiliary verb** to tell us that something is happening **now**, or going on over time.

To be

I **am** dancing.
You **are** dancing.
He/She **is** dancing.
They/We **are** dancing.

Rewrite these sentences, which use an **auxiliary verb**. Start each sentence with a capital letter.

at are party. They dancing the

_____

_____

is the party. She enjoying

_____

The **verb** 'have' also acts as an **auxiliary verb** to form a different tense.

To have

I **have** eaten.
You **have** eaten.
He/She **has** eaten.
They/We **have** eaten.

Rewrite these sentences, which use an **auxiliary verb.** Start each sentence with a capital letter.

eaten all. He it has _____

_____

have eaten food. They all the _____

_____

Circle the **auxiliary verbs** in the sentences you have written.

To find out more about **auxiliary verbs** and using the **tenses** that go with them, you'll need our book on Tenses in this series.

Well done!

Sentences

All **sentences** have a **subject** (often a noun) and a **verb** (an action). The **subject** tells you who, or what, is doing the **action**.

Draw a line between the **subjects** and **actions** to make the **sentence**.

Subject	Verb (action)
The rocket	is roaring.
The bird	is flying.
The gate	is zooming.
The dinosaur	is creaking.

Write your own **sentence** about this duck.

The duck is _____.

To make longer sentences, add an **object** (usually another noun). The **object** comes after the **verb** and tells us who or what is receiving the **action**.

The dog is watching the ball.

subject	verb	object

Label these sentences to show which is the **subject**, **verb** and **object**.

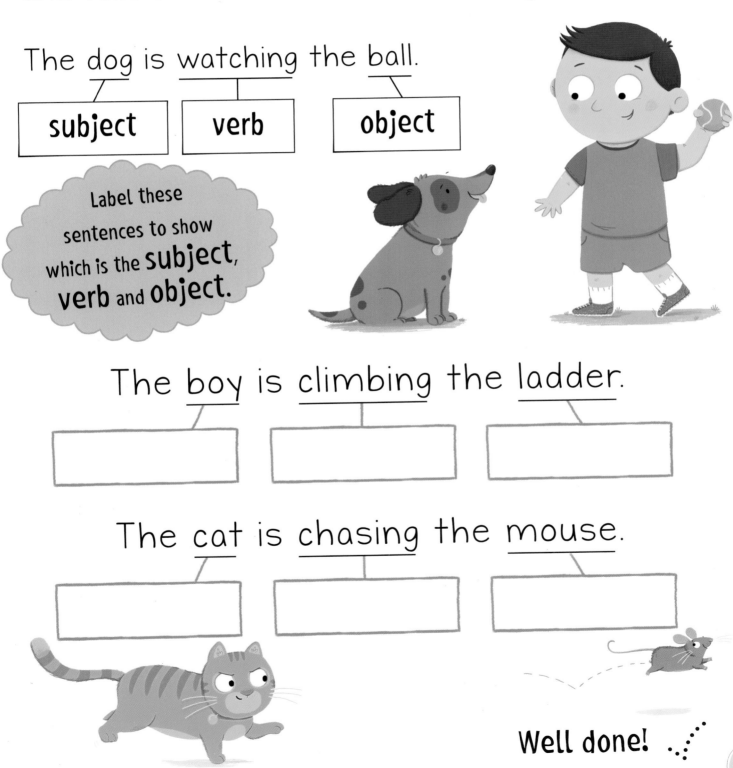

The boy is climbing the ladder.

The cat is chasing the mouse.

Well done!

First, second and third person

Sentences can be written as if by different people:

First person = 'I' or 'we'
I am writing.   **We** are writing.

Second person = 'you'   **You** are writing.

Third person = 'he', 'she' or 'they'
He is writing.   **She** is writing.   **They** are writing.

Complete these sentences using the **third person.**

Use the **second person** to describe what someone near you is doing now.

_____ listening to music.

_____ driving her car.

_____ riding his horse.

_____ packing their bags.

First, second and third person

Instructions are often written in the **second person** with the **verb** at the beginning.

Get off the train at the next station.

LONDON

Turn right at the next junction.

Try writing **instructions** about what to do before you go to school.

Wake up. Get out of bed.

TOWN CENTRE

Use the **second person** to tell someone how to brush their teeth.

Well done!

Commas

Commas separate things in a list and show a pause in a **sentence**. You don't need a **comma** before the word 'and'.

The children are playing on the swings, seesaw, roundabout and slide, then they will go home at dinner time.

separates the list

shows a pause

Add **commas** to these sentences.

She is packing her hat sunglasses and towel then she will leave for her holiday tomorrow.

He is eating eggs bacon sausages and toast then he will go to school.

Speech marks show when a person is speaking. They can also be called **inverted commas**.

"I am walking to school," he said.
"I am going by train," she replied.

The words '**said**' and '**replied**' are **verbs**.

Add the **speech marks** and the **commas** to these sentences.

She is going to the zoo with Matt Rosie Sam and Tia he said. They will see lions penguins giraffes and monkeys then have a picnic in the afternoon she replied.

Well done!

Adverbs

An **adverb** gives more information about the **verb**. It tells you when, where or how something is happening.

She is playing tennis **now**.

Try using one of these 'when' **adverbs** to finish this sentence.

later   today   tomorrow

He is playing football   .

Try using one of these 'where' **adverbs** to finish this sentence.

He is waiting **downstairs**.

upstairs   inside   outside

We are going   .